Broken Horizons

Also by Richard Jackson

Poems
*Part of the Story*
*Worlds Apart*
*Alive All Day*
*Falling Stars* (Limited Edition)
*Svetovi Narazen* (Slovenia)
*Heart's Bridge* (Limited Edition)
*Heartwall*
*Half Lives*
*Unauthorized Autobiography*
*Resonance*
*Retrievals*
*Resonancia* (Barcelona)
*Out of Place*
*Traversings* (with Robert Vivian)

Translations
*Last Poems: Selected Poems of Pascoli* (Italian, with Susan Thomas,
Deborah Brown)
*Potovanje Sonca* (Journey of the Sun) by Alexsander Peršola
(Slovene)

Chapbooks
*Fifties*
*Cesare Pavese: The Woman in the Land* (translation)
*Greatest Hits 1980-2004*

Criticism
*The Dismantling of Time in Contemporary American Poetry*
*Acts of Mind: Interviews with Contemporary Poets*

Anthologies
*The Fire Under The Moon: Contemporary Slovene Poetry*
*Double Vision: Four Slovenian Poets* (with Aleš Debeljak)
*A Bridge of Voices* (online e-book, with Barbara Carlson)
*The Heart's Many Doors: American Poets Respond to Metka Krašovec's
Images Responding to Emily Dickinson*

Edited Books
Tomaž Šalamun, *Ko vdre senca/When the Shadow Breaks*
Iztok Osojnik: *Selected Poems*
Iztok Osojnik, *Wagner (co-editing with others)*

# Broken Horizons

Poems

Richard Jackson

Press 53
Winston-Salem

Press 53, LLC
PO Box 30314
Winston-Salem, NC 27130


First Edition

Silver Concho Poetry Series
edited by Pamela Uschuk and William Pitt Root

Cover design by Kevin Morgan Watson

Cover art, "*Vigilje*," (*Vigils*, Acrylic on Canvas, 135x160 cm)
Copyright © 1995 by Metka Krašovec,
used by permission of the artist.

Author photo by Terri Harvey

Library of Congress Control Number
2017964652



Printed on acid-free paper
ISBN 978-1-941209-72-1

*for Terri*

The author wishes to thank the editors of the publications where
the following poems first appeared:

*B O D Y* (Prague)
    The Mudpuddle
    Traces
    The Twitter Novels

*Brilliant Corners*
    Elegy: Reading Keats and Listening to Clifford Brown
    Listening to the Band at Bar Prulček
    Like Cemetery Blues

*Chattanooga Times*
    Chattanooga, 16 July 2015

*Cutthroat: A Journal of the Arts*
    Complaint of the Muse
    It Is if You Say It Is

*Eco Theo*
    Micah's Prophecy

*Georgia Review*
    Easy
    Invisible Star Maps

*Heart's Many Doors* (anthology)
    The Doors of the Heart

*North American Review*
    Floating

*Speak for Forests Falling* (anthology)
    Dawn on Amelia Island

*Truth To Power* (anthology)
    Litany of the Self's Broken Horizons

*Wildness*
    Spooky Action at a Distance
    The Secrets of the Imagination

# Contents

There I was, unable to say what I'd seen
But I was happy, and my happiness made others happy

   —Marvin Bell
    "Unless It Was Courage," *Nightworks*


I feel a slackening in the vertical axis of the earth.
Galactic axis, the one we are used to,
breaks. I don't know anymore what I see.

   —Tomaž Šalamun
    "Ridges of Aromatic," *The Book for My Brother*

# I

## *KEEPING WATCH*

*how long we*
*stood there nailed to the spot,*
*hand in hand, expectant,*
*as though anything could tell us where we were.*

—Phillip Levine
"Albion," *The Last Shift*

# Easy

A few constellations begin to poke through the fabric
of the sky. Bits of moonlight rub against the water.
It's easy to imagine how the leftover light at dusk
leaves us wandering through our own dreams
trying to pick out what's real. It's easy to see
the man at the railing of the Walnut Street Bridge as
a jumper. Just think of the way his lost past sits like
a squatter on his heart, how whatever he dreamt
has gone on without him. Is that why he has tossed
a few coins in the sax player's case? Nightbirds in
the trestle above him keep repeating things he can't
say himself. There's the mold in the fridge, the shadeless
lamp. You can imagine the rest. There's always a note
someone's saved.

Do you think I am making this up because
it's so easy? It may be that our words colonize our feelings,
that we know everything by its opposite. *Why is there
something rather than nothing?* the philosophers always ask.
We really can't escape what we dream. I wish I could
know if the man were going to jump, but what would I do?

I've come here to listen to the music, not to write this.
Words have their own agenda and it doesn't include us.
So it's easy to see how our histories get lost the way
those plastic bags that were once filled with items we've
long forgotten accumulate against the chain link fence.
Each star we can name is surrounded by its own darkness.
There's the river's darkness in every history we know.
Not so many years ago they hung two Black men,
Ed Johnson in 1906 and Alfred Blount in 1893 on this
bridge continuing, as it were, after Columbus who
enslaved and let be raped, over a quarter million
Taino Indians in Hispanola. And now they are
uncovering another mass grave in Mexico, more
in the Sudan, opening like trap doors to the soul,
and it would be easy to file that away and write about

something personal and forget everything that's happened.
It's easy to stand by like the bystanders who recorded
the assault on Gilbert Estrada, aged 51, in San Diego
on their cell phones. In truth, they hovered over
their own shadows.

                    There's a hive of stars gathering
above the bridge. I would like to find the words
to make sure the man only looks longingly at the way
night has begun to deepen itself in the river. It's easy
to drown yourself in words that drift out of your past.
*Don't play what's there, play what's not there,*
Miles Davis once said. And maybe that's the answer.
We have our Being in others, Paul Tillich wrote.
When a fish splashes the water with light we want
to take it as a sign.

                    I've said about all I can.
I'll keep watch until the Bridge is cleared.
Venus has sunk below the far hill. *'Round Midnight,*
the sax player starts up again just to keep breathing.
Our own lives are littered with darkened voices.
*Why Was I Born,* played Kenny Burrell and John Coltrane,
and the night blows over. It's a question you have
to answer on the bridge. It's not easy, but it's up to you.

# Invisible Star Maps

Remembering my stepdaughter, Kari Harvey (1982–2016)

*We know that we have passed out of death into life.*
—1 John 3:14

Wherever we go we leave a thumbprint of the soul.
Ghosts of words we never said fill the rooms we leave.
This is why we have to touch what the missing have touched.
In the morning we see how the orb weaver has mapped
the last light, and how the Gazania flower opens its colors
to morning.

*The heart maps these stories where the clocks*
*seem unsure of themselves.*

Now the heron lifting suddenly
from the shore leaves the story I need to write. I believe
these things the way the tree believes in the dark world
of its roots, or how the brook remembers its origins upstream,
how we know where we are by the clang of a buoy through fog.

*The heart maps invisible traces that are fog on my eyeglasses.*
*What we don't see is, in the end, the shore we are headed for.*

Medieval map makers drew what might happen at each turn
on their journey, or made perfect picture worlds that existed
only in myths because they knew every place is a storehouse
of possibility, every place is a time that has yet to occur,
an unreadable history of the heart. In Syria the smudges
on aerial photographs are the mass graves of the missing.

*The heart maps paths the survivors still take through abandoned*
*minefields. What we don't hear is, in the end, the distant rumor of dawn.*

In the nineteenth century spectral photos returned the dead
to us. Now, just these old Polaroids, snapshots of some family
gathering. If only they could show me what lies beyond us.
Strabo (64BC-24AD) traced his spherical star maps
onto his earth map to bring us closer to heaven. Opicicni drew

his mystic world as graffiti on city walls, the Mediterranean
here as queens, saints, gryphons and other mysteries to be explored.

*The heart maps the empty sky between those constellations.*

It's true that all these facts are ways to avoid my own losses,
as if history erased the many histories it is made of.

*What we don't see is, in the end, what the stars are hiding.*

We want to put ourselves into the maps our dead have followed.
We want to read the elusive messages the wind writes
with ocean spray. We want to see heaven pivot on its axis
with every memory that breaks the surface. Here the moon
drags the dawn behind it. Eternity hides in the lost meanings
of these words. There are losses so deep, loves so—I can't say.

*The heart maps itself with symbols so no one else can read it.*

There are reflections on the water that are her own dreams.
There are moments when her shadows disguise themselves as first light.
Above us, the plane has already left where its engine sounds.

*What we don't hear is, in the end, the silence between heartbeats.*

There are losses so deep. Now the sky is weighted down
with memories. Losses so deep. Even our shadows desert us.
I see, then, whatever we know we know by its absence—lives
that once travelled the old roads now barely perceptible
depressions through the woods, the invisible particles we take
on faith because of the paths they leave on a laboratory screen,
the odor of bear or deer we cross on a trail, the lives that continue
between flashes of last night's fireflies.

>                              *What we don't touch*
> *touches us, which is why we turn back as if there were someone*
> *there, which is why we turn back each time.*

And this morning,
above us, invisible stars the daylight hides begin to map for us,
secretly, new paths our hearts had seemed to despair of,—those
vapor trails that linger longer than they are supposed to, the wake
of the boat that echoes perhaps endlessly, shore to shore,—if only
we can believe in them without ever seeing where they are.

# Listening to the Band At Bar Prulček, In Ljubljana, Slovenia

*Some secrets can't quit /memory fast enough*
— William Matthews, "Bucket's Got a Hole In It"

*When I was alive,* we say as Počeni Škafi (Broken Bucket)
strikes up *When the Saints Go Marchin In,* because it seems
we are living on one of those multi universes that float,
as the science says, simultaneously, like bubbles beyond
our own. So, for a while we can smuggle our own feelings into
whatever tune comes next. For a while, that is, we can just
forget the bombings in Manchester and Baghdad. For
a while we can seem to live on one of those alternate worlds.
So then it's *My Bucket's Got a Hole In It,* their signature tune,
meaning the way our beer and memories escape so easily
but also the porous bucket as broken condom. At least
that's what the crowd yells, and maybe it is only in music
that our contradictory worlds really appear. Maybe
it really is the music of the spheres that holds us all
together. Maybe those swallows circling the outside patio
really are arranging themselves as notes arriving from
another age. So it seems it is also 25 years ago, another
side of town, listening to the bar's crackling speakers voice
Louis Armstrong's relaxed phrasings on *Bucket* which seems
to hold the exploding world together just south of here.
Jack Teagarden's trombone sliding with Earl Hine's
trumpeting piano over each atrocity, not to blot them out
but to provide some hope. So it seems the day gives away
nothing it needs to keep being the day. So it seems for
the couples rising now to dance as the quartet's trumpet
calls them to the floor. Even those swallows around the
patio seem to be keeping time, though we know it can't
be kept. And now the band responds by shifting into Swing.
It is not enough to understand this life if you only live it once.

# Like Cemetery Blues

*I don't want no drummer. I set the tempo.*
— Bessie Smith

It is possible nothing happened. It is possible
the dawn's red shawl draped over the hills is
not a warning. The early hummingbirds dart
about indecisively. Doubts collect on the rough
undersides of leaves. Even the mockingbird
can't settle on one voice. There were images
last night that struck like the momentary visions
revealed by bomb flashes. It's possible it was only
a nightmare. Flocks of memories fly off to
return unrecognized. Reality is undergoing
another rehearsal. That's why it is possible
to forget the albino children of Mozambique
sold for body parts. It is possible the boy
riding his bike through the minefield will
make it. *I'm going down to the cemetery*
*'cause the world is all wrong* sang Bessie Smith
in 1923, the same year *Popular Science* praised
the Eugenics program in Kansas. It was
Jimmy Jones's block chords marching steady
with her to the grave's edge. This morning
I am reading the poems of Tonči Marović
who believed he'd turned into a sparrow
that visited him on the windowsill of his prison
cell in Split in 1991 a few months before
his soul flew off. These images are the lizards
darting into crevices in his stone walls.
It is possible that Bessie Smith knew about
the women being sterilized in Baltimore as
she sang, because all these images are connected.
This morning her voice is trying to make sense
of all this terror as it plays in the background.
What we know are points on a compass
that has no needle. It is possible either despair
or love, weeping or song will win out here.
The river here doesn't listen to what we say—

it has its own words for what hides beneath
the surface. Every death sticks in the throat.
In the years she sang the Black men of Tuskegee
were a control group treated for their syphilis.
They were told only that they had "bad blood."
The shadows we cast sometimes paint a picture
that has nothing to do with what we want to see.
Bessie tried to live inside the one perfect song
she never found. After the wreck, she lay for hours
by the side of a Mississippi road and never woke.
The owl's cry slept in the grass. I believe it was a tune
she knew. It was a dream of stars not yet born.
Do you think I am crazy dreaming all this?
It is the song we must continue to sing. *It's
a Long Old Road but I Know I'm Gonna Find
the End,* she'd sing a few years before the end,
but she never meant where *The Devil's Gonna
Get You.* This morning the road leads off like
a prophet. The river keeps its own time which has
nothing to do with what I hear her singing. There,
a mother duck looks back at the ducklings who are
following her like notes on a staff. Sometimes music
changes the color of the air, sometimes it questions
the very solidness of the earth we walk upon.
It is possible she sensed the magnolia blossoms
swaying above her as she lay waiting in the dark.
Above her the mockingbird had already adopted
her voice. For a moment the sky opened as a whole note.
For a moment it was all jay and robin and sparrow.
For a moment the earth responded as one block note.
This morning I think it is possible to believe anything.
It is possible we are all sparrows on a windowsill
waiting for the song that lifts us beyond ourselves
because *the world is all wrong*, and because we still believe.

# Litany of the Self's Broken Horizon

*The finite has no genuine being.*
*There soon creeps in the misconception of already*
*knowing before you know.*
　　　　—GWF Hegel

When our dreams drive off into bottomless ditches.
When the moon refuses to shine on the tombstones.
When the presumptuous clocks abandon memory.
When the sky fades out before dawn has a chance.
When the shadows break camp and march on us.
When a mine sprouts through the earth at someone's step.
It doesn't matter if we hang our words from steeple
to steeple. If love breaks the rung on the ladder below it.
If the curtain of the sky slips from its window.
There's a carload of futures circling the block.
There's a wrinkled emphysemiac at the emergency
room blowing smoke into a plastic liter bottle so he can
breathe again. There's another in his underwear calling to
to the angels who don't listen. Down the street there's a rusted
metal sign, its words worn out, clanging its message
to an improbable future. It was Hegel who knew that everything
we know is contradicted by something else we know.
I have never revealed my dream of the charred waves.
I have no idea where the mastless sails took me.
The only horizons are the ones we have passed.
The world is everything it is about to be.
There is no sense in becoming the grave robbers of our failures.
At every moment we have reached the middle of our lives.
You turn your head but it wasn't you who was being called.
The wearer of a bomb vest invests in every compass point.
Every slogan has its own hive of lies that roam about freely.
Our windows fog with theory. Mallarmé knew the mind is
a spider web whose ideas are trapped by chance. As when
our words are known by the bomb craters they leave.
When our futures begin to betray the pasts we cherished.
When every stone contains countless colliding asteroids.
When we fight the border wars between desire and memory.
When we find ourselves strangers in our own minds.
That's when our hearts hang from the sweetest fruit trees.
When each word becomes an orchestra with no conductor.

When the flocks of our ideas fly off in all directions.
When truth is the scandal the nightingale sings about.
When the tree frogs know more than we will ever know.
When the old truths no longer open the soul's locks.
When one lovely war replaces another. When the stars begin
to flatter one another for favors. When one god promises
its candle wax will not flow like tears, when one skeleton
spies on another skeleton, when their gossip comes law.
How many bodies must be splattered on how many
café walls to arrive at a truth that will soon fail everyone.
Someone has been knocking at the door of my dream.
Every word becomes eventually its own prison.
Therefore, the galaxy turns cartwheels without end.
Therefore, the trees bow down to the wind they never see.
Therefore, I disguise myself as myself while I am
waiting to see whatever the stars might hatch into.

# Elegy: Reading Keats and Listening
# to Clifford Brown

Kari Harvey, 1982–2016

The moon is sleepwalking through the trees. A stupor
of fog slides drowsily over the channel's surface. Two herons
rise out of it with an enthusiasm of wings. Asteroid 2016103
has played a cosmic blues with us as it shadows our orbit,
now behind, now ahead of us. Some astronomers call it
*Love.* "What Is This Thing Called Love" Clifford Brown blew
at Basin Street, February 1956. In a few months his car would
tumble in eighth notes down an embankment. A few months
from his own death Keats would improvise a new ending
for Spenser's *Faerie Queene,* his last verse. He wanted,
he said, to carry the moon in his pocket. He, too, would bear
his secret like a hairline fracture of the heart. He's buried with
his love's unread letters. *Joy Spring,* Clifford would write for his wife.

Here the leaves drip with dew, the cicadas improvise upon
each other's melodies. Trumpet flowers want to play to the clouds.
Sometimes the words for things sound louder than the things.
Too many of them seem to be crowding into this moment.
Brownie would manipulate chords so he wouldn't have to
stay in a single present. I think he knew how time frays into
other times. You have to live in "uncertainty and doubt,"
wrote Keats, you have to lose your identity in the music,
you have to "choose between despair and Energy," he added.

It was with that energy Clifford chose to attack each note
that seems now to breach like a dolphin. He'd race and swim
around his horn, Dizzie said. Is there a water beneath
the water, a sky behind the sky? A note between the notes
we don't hear? The moon is gradually wearing out. We don't
see those asteroids that burn up their secrets in the atmosphere
and, if we do, we name them shooting stars. No matter.
It was all blues and gospel at their ends. *I'll Remember April,*
Brownie goes on. We all have too many postcard memories,
too many slips of paper we can no longer read. Every idea
disappears behind its word the way one landscape gives way
to another over millions of years. There's always a bigger picture.

How many lives like these flick out of the corners of our eyes
before we can describe them? It is our shadows that tell us what
or who has been missing. At night we know there are boats
on the water by their running lights. Even Moses couldn't describe
the backside of God. "Heard melodies are sweet, but those unheard
are sweeter," wrote Keats. Finally, now, the mockingbirds begin
their own improvisations. They can tell you everything about the past.
I have no idea why they choose which sound to riff off. There are
so many unused words I have pocketed out of sight, so many
things I should have said or done. So many. How often the world
seems to arrive too late, that single note that hangs unheard. The secret
of this poem is the name I choose not to voice, the imperceptible sound
of the trumpet valve, the distant hum of galaxy M4 we never hear,
the silent paths those Jesus bugs leave on the water. Beneath them a few
bubbles poke the surface as if to explore another world. Above them
spiders are prophets because they weave a future between branches
they can see. A heron drinks the reflection of a plane. It doesn't know
like Keats' Lamia, which world it should enter. The sky's membrane
pulses with unplayed notes. "I always made an awkward bow,"
wrote Keats at the end. *Choose Now* is how Brownie's session ends.

# The Story

We never know where the paths of the sunlight begin
or where they end. The first sundial was called a Gnomon,
meaning *one who knows*, from the 35th century Mesopotamia,
and still used by African Bushmen.

                                      This morning I feel I have
come from a place I no longer remember. The light seems
to genuflect on the roadside. There's a ditch here but it carries
its own stories from somewhere near the top of the ridge.
The darkness won't abandon its secret places. Sometimes
it seems we are like those characters in math problems
running towards the rear of a train that's rushing forward.
Where we were is never where we were. Our maps and
stories are made of mist.

                               In one version it must have been
an important place, what those few worn letters
that were left tried to announce on the brick
wall beside the vacant lot. And that scraggly tree that still
shades the old men who gather there by day, and beside
the fire barrel by night, what attracts all those birds
gathering like broken smoke in the branches? Or it is that
their leaves are made of birdsong. They speak in a language
we know before we hear it. But by the time we arrived
the story had come to its natural close.

                                   In another version
the dew is still heavy on the grass. For a moment you are
asleep in my heart. What more can I ask for? I am rocking
inside your breaths. I have turned into the words you whisper.
When I speak to you, I clothe my heart with your heart.
When you tighten and tremble into love, these dreams
wander into distant fields and leave no tracks. I have
never been so lost, I have never been so certain of
where I am. Inside you, it seemed as if you were
quivering with the stars that had faded away billions
of years ago to be reborn in another galaxy.

But you have
your own stories, and your own way of saying what
you miss. Sometimes our versions are dim lights
at the far ends of a street or alley.

How easy it is
to lose ourselves in our own stories. Wherever we are
we replace what is missing. How unbelievable
that we have not devoured each other the way some lost
galaxies have swallowed each other since the beginning
of time, or the way the mantis devours its mate so lovingly.

# The Secrets of Imagination

I imagined you said the cicadas, afraid we would overhear
their secrets, stop as we approach. I imagined you said
they are planning, as Plato thought, our future. I was, sorry,
prying, like those doctors in 1822 who examined the insides
of Alexis St Martin through the bullet wound in his stomach
that healed with a permanent opening. We are such mysteries
to ourselves. Tonight a few orphaned stars announce themselves
again. A straggling cloud loses its way behind the trees.
How often our own dreams struggle against gravity. I imagined
the man who'll clean the park in the morning collecting scraps
of paper out of which he invents the story of his life. He too
looks through the world we know to the world we don't know.
I imagined the five dimensional world the scientists say cloaks ours
so that we can never really measure what we see. This morning
I surprised two raccoons who turned and disappeared back
towards the mulch pile. A moment later the mother dashed out
from hiding in the bushes when I passed out of range. The air
seemed to hold, and then dissolve, her presence. But tonight
the moon seems reluctant to reveal anything. The usual dusk
light is dismissive. A streetlight flickers. A vapor trail breaks up
on the first stars. I imagine the cicadas say one thing to us,
another to themselves. I can't imagine how many worlds
lie between what we don't say and what we do. I don't know
what happens to all those memories we hold. I imagine they linger
in the places we have been. Where the raccoons disappeared
soldiers fled a battle on the ridge a hundred and fifty years ago
leaving behind not only buttons and buckles for metal detectors
but their spirits that haunt the woods. Or their dreams are fossils.
Now a trellis of sounds hovers over us again. In Sansepolcro
the eyes in Pierro della Francesca's *Resurrection of Christ* tracked
us wherever we stood in the gallery. It was as if we were urged
to invent another life than what we knew. From where we stand now
our own lives watch us from the shadows that perch among the trees.
Whatever they say is said in the language of flickering leaves.
Tomorrow the raccoons will know to keep together. It was just
a failure of imagination. The cicadas know everything we failed to love
tells us what we need to love. It is the secret we all share beyond words.
Or this: we carry inside us a hidden life that we hold only to share,
like the dove the man trying to cross the border in Texas kept
in his pocket, saying, when captured, it was for luck, and from love.

# One Way to Dream

for Ata and Christina

*No one sews a piece of unshrunk cloth on an*
*Old cloak; otherwise, the patch pulls away from*
*It, the new from the old, and a worse tear is made.*
—Mark 2:21

A robin dips into a puddle and flutters the water
from its wings. Above him, the fog seems to glow
with a billboard's neon. He's in an abandoned lot
of broken glass that mirrors forgotten images.
There are so many unexplored galaxies behind our
eyelids. One sailboat capsizes then rights itself
on the river. A city falcon rising into the fog
must think it has reached heaven. I am on my way
to the airport passing store mannequins that have
their own dreams. The dreams we have dressed
ourselves in will need to be patched. Which is
what love is—dreaming ourselves into all new and
possible forms of love, the way a flame quivers like
a leaf that itself is dreaming it has become a flame.

# Floating

*What is there left to say about this free floating I?*
—Paul Ricoeur, *Oneself as Another*

As when the raccoons approached and walked by as if
we were not there, or when the sudden overcast
wiped away our shadows, or when we were reading
how the universe keeps expanding but leaves us behind,
we began to think of ourselves like those mirages
that waver off the desert floor, maybe the invisible
force that drives the tumbleweed and kicks up
dust devils though they have nothing to do with real
devils which is the point after all, wondering here
how real we are not to be noticed, if we have been
distorted like those fun house mirrors, or like the fish
who are never where we think because of the light's
refraction, fractioning us, because we have forgotten
whatever it is we thought we were, what seems now
to float across the yard like those dandelion seeds
themselves too early, not heeding the calendar, or us,
which brings us to the point here, the women separated
from their children at the border as if they were not
real, only blown weeds or mirages in someone's scope
becoming smaller and smaller as we all are, knowing this,
sitting here letting history blow us wherever, the whole
universe watching us shrink into our own distances.

# The Twitter Novels

*The name of the story will be Time,*
*But you must not pronounce its name.*
　　　　　　—Robert Penn Warren, *Audubon*

Sometimes I am just a stick churning hopelessly under a waterfall
looking for a way out of your dream. Sometimes I have to admit
the stunning morning light against Paul's house is perishable. Every
sentence here is a trial balloon for a story I should have written.
The harvest moon last night with Jupiter pasted humbly beneath it
stood for everything I know. How few know the difference between
the sound of a star and a planet. A star's life is inversely proportional
to its mass which is why so much of what we see is the light cast out
eons ago like desperate refugees. What if we each live in our own
times and only see the people whose times touch our own? Orchids
are the oldest flowering plant with hundreds of species, each
with its own pollinating insect. Who was I when I wrote that?
There are so many things we can't explain: the car alarm that rang
for an hour the other night that seemed to come from nowhere,
the woman who kept a pack of starving dogs, the kind of cruelty
that posts a roommate's gay encounter on the internet until the victim
jumps from the George Washington bridge, or what was left
of the village after the Sudanese soldiers left just a few limbs
hissing like sap from logs. Sometimes I don't know how to live
in the world. Sometimes the morning light is pulled from
its sheath. Each sentence I write whispers like a tweet, a grace
note reminding us that we never listen long enough to understand
each other, that we stand in the dark corner of a canvas the artist
never finished. Whatever happened to the faith that moved
mountains? Sometimes you have to smuggle your feelings across
well guarded borders. It's been a while since I saw my own face
in the mirror. Why is there always this scent of sorrow,
the shattered windshield of memory as it approaches silently?
If only we could decant the night. If only the day would rise
as geese in perfect order from the pond. Then we might know
the name of the world. The weight of the owl is beyond
imagining. Time shrinks like a cheap fabric. Where are we?
Plato thought the real was what we could never touch.
How thin is the curtain between ourselves and our worlds:
sometimes I can't stand the crying of stars any longer.
If only I could decipher the red spots on the insides of my eyelids.

You would think I have lived long enough to tell you what I mean.
All I see are these metaphors straggling behind what they were
supposed to say, heat lightning that connects a few syllables
by chance. It is in those moments that time sways on the broken
branch of a tree, it is in those moments I understand how
the earth groans to tell us what the heart knows, but fears to say.

# II

## *I IS AN OTHER*

When all things lay in the midst of silence
then there descended down into me from on high...a secret word.

—*Wisdom* 18:14
quoted by Meister Eckhart, Sermon 101

# Joseph's Dream

That deep in the pit I could see the hidden dreams
of daylight stars. If I listened carefully, I could hear
the earth's plates grumbling. I didn't know why.
Every once in a while a grudging wind might twist
its way down to me. Every once in a while a raindrop
would leave its thumbprint in the mud. I learned, then,
that our real histories lie in wait in the shadows.
My own brothers tried to kill or sell me, you know
the story. Revenge crumbled from the dirt walls.
But it's true, I was unfair. I thought to imprison
them. I dreamt the sheaves and stars bowed
down to me. My own words became my chains.
I was ashamed. What I can't decipher is your own
cavernous dreams. They have no meanings that don't
spread out like the tracks of a frightened herd towards
wars, rapes, beheadings and the refugees from the everyday
selling of lives. You thought you could put the moon
in a prison. You called arrogance by the name of
practicality. The books you held sacred you refused
to follow. Pretty soon another day is out of reach.
What will you dream when your words are forgotten?
This morning I watched as a stray dog settled into sleep
among the worn headstones. I do not know whether
he was remembering or forgetting. I think we have to
burrow deep into our own dreams, into the pits of
our worst desires. We have to gather every syllable
in search of a truer meaning. Sometimes our dreams
seek sanctuary in what we can't say. Why can't we
clothe our hearts in each others' hearts? My dream
eddies out of the coves and inlets of these words. Here,
a firefly lights, now and then, the ashes of a dead star.

# David's Lost Psalm

Winter's net of black branches has begun to haul in
a few buds and leaves. There's nothing to explain
our desire to embrace all that surrounds us. A sudden
sun has made the statues glisten. I remember my own
age of cries as dreadful as yours. We all desired
a story different than the one we lived. I sang
whatever was true, however painful or torturous,
not to dwell in those valleys but to climb out of them.
No one wanted to remember the wars, the captivity,
the rapes. No one wanted to remember that we too
did unspeakable crimes. Now your own stories are
so light they drift away like milkweed looking for
some better ground. There isn't any, there never is.
The moon's scarred face gives us back our souls.
Saul thought I would drift away, then tried to kill me.
I forgave him as I forgave myself. My own faults now
crumble like pages of a forgotten passion. All I know is
that memory is a place that is nowhere, which is why
we can retrieve the lives we never lived. Each song is
a woods where the paths return always to the beginning.
I sang to invent what I could not remember, or to remember
what I could not invent. It was the only way to let my soul
glisten as if it knew. Here a few deer step out of the woods.
The cornstalk stubble has been burnt away. The cemetery
stones are telling only a part of the story but that seems
enough. A sudden wind nudges the statues awake.

# Ruth's Hope

*Judge not, that you be not judged. For with what judgment you judge, you will be judged; and with the measure you use, it will be measured back to you.*
—Matthew 7:1, NKJV

Today it would be Jordan. I would wear a head scarf.
It would be the same sun eating the dirt, making thorns
of the air. I left my people yes, but love them still, while
their lands are bulldozed, the same lands you once
exiled them to, where my husband lay. Because you left
the fallen grain for the poor I went to gather it. It is
that same dust that seasons our food, the same wind
that is sandpaper on the face. You could map my journey
by its tendrils of pain. I was still a foreigner. I was
ready to pull down the clouds around me. But I knew
that the new belief was tolerance. What has happened?
The birds and snakes have become planes and tanks.
The words you once used to embrace have changed into
words that will strangle you. There is no other ending.
My own road took me to a Bethlehem before yours.
My own road took me to a husband whose words
cloaked me. This morning a sparrow pecking uselessly
for seeds would not give up, its wings fluttering like
a heart. It paid no attention to the contrails of jets.
The face of the desert has a look this evening that
I would like to call home, that I would like to call love.

# Francis' Prayer

What I never understood was that I never owned
even myself. I used to listen to the river trying to claw
its way back to the hills over the rapids. I used to walk
only in the shadows that seemed to spread like thrown
cloaks in front of me. Everything we own is owned by
something else. In the end we'd fight for the dew
that collects on the fallen, the clouds that seem to shade
an enemy, even the faint tracks the robber would leave
in the alleyway.

         And now? One morning someone blows
himself up or sends a missile down some chimney just
to own the breath he'll soon exhale. Our words are
vapor as the Preacher says. We have to remember how
the wind blows away the wind. We have to escape
the mind's broken bridges.  We have to let our hearts
empty themselves in the sea.

         One day I could feel
the sun burn into my hands and side. Another day
it seemed the devils leaving Arezzo were shadows
of stars. There are so many things we see that have
no words, so many words written in invisible ink.

We have to learn the language of birds which is prayer.
There is always another heart within the heart, for
what we own is never what we have, what we love
is never what we own

         just as the woman in Nigeria knew
caring for the friends whose bodies had become pustules
and leaked their own blood, putting on their wounds like
a cloak, like Job, like more than all the love we can own.

# Paul's Lesson

They say every belief is a prison but I have known
prisons. They say the soul is a punctured balloon.
At the sound of a trumpet they arm themselves
with hate. Their crusades became histories of grief.
Their own souls became coffins. Who could begin
again in a world like that? I travel still in chains.
My journeys have never ended. That's why you are
still reading. That's why your faith still knocks
on the door. Forget the messengers who have forgotten
the meaning of their words. I remember the storms at sea,
the fear that drove men towards the unspeakable.
Sometimes the rain fell in needles. Sometimes the air was
charged with revenge. Yes, it was difficult to believe
through those nights dressed in despair. It was difficult.
I was ready to pronounce my own sentence. I was ready
to hold the sword or light the flame myself. The way
out is the way in. And now you ask about the beheadings
and rapes, the suicide bombers, the refugees moving like
a dust storm over the face of the earth. It is a hard thing,
what I ask in return. You can kill what you hate until
there is no one left in the vacuum around you. You can
poison the air with your own bombs. But you can also
turn away from those shadows of oblivion. The only real
borders are the ones we create in our hearts. You might want
to curse the moon. You might want to behead those who would
behead you. When you lift the sword above your head
remember what you have raised above you, how every
killing is a form of suicide. And how every love is a seed
but that what it brings is nothing you asked for, nothing
you didn't already have waiting behind the doors of your heart.

# Balaam's Prophecy

Yes, we were always handcuffed to our old habits.
Yes, to see the truth is to look through tracing paper.
In the end, my life was worth the same as roadkill.
Because of me the sky seems pockmarked with stars.
Ravens turn the trees black. Our sins are laid out like
fish at the market. There were signs, yes, but me, I
prophesized a whole nation against itself and thousands
fell by the plague. I had hoped no one would remember.
It wasn't only what I believed, but what I didn't believe.
It wasn't only what I did, but what I didn't do. I should have
helped the Moabites to change. I should have heard
an Angel and not a donkey. What you don't want
to see is not a reason to close your eyes. And you,
your own bullets turn the air to lace and then you want
to sell the lace. You peel away the souls of the poor.
You dress the rich in fine excuses. You aren't any
different. Your past plays in the background like
a drummer's soft brushing. What I was told to tell you
I told to Barak—that the world you are about to make is
not the world you think, that the vaults of your ears are closed,
the doors of your eyes locked shut, that the corridors of
your hearts are hordes for your profits, that your souls are
laced with blind excuses. In the end, you have to choose.
A vulture sweeps its black hand over the far field.
A dove alights on the garden wall as if remembering the flood.

# Isaiah's Judgement

*The vision of all this has become for you like words of*
*a sealed document.*
—Isaiah 29:11

For three years I walked your roads clothed only
with the wind which was a sign for all you'll lose.
In the meantime you tossed your beliefs out like worn
rags, and dressed yourself in words made of gossamer.
What I spoke glowed like coals from my lips but you
saw only darkness. What I heard could send you back
to caves in the rocks. What I saw you would not believe.
Where is justice when you abandon the poor to shells
of buildings, the homeless to tents hidden in woods
by polluted streams and the tunnels beneath your cities?
When you refuse the immigrants you refuse yourselves.
When you fear the lies of tyrants you fear yourselves.
It is not too late. You have to listen the way the grass
listens to the wind, the way the roots listen for water.
Even the silences of space contain the words whispered
from the beginning of time. It is not too late to cast off
the shadows you wear like armor. It is not too late.
There, in the street, the face of a child is clothed
in the dirt of words you use for her. She sells herself
for whatever she can get. It is not enough to only see
what your eyes see, what your ears hear, for you must
listen to the sound of the light striking the earth, see
the eagle's cry cutting across the valley, touch the scent
of morning flowers. All this I have said before and yet
already your own words are insects eating holes
in the cloaks with which you have clothed your own hearts.

# Micah's Prophecy

II Chronicles 18

Time subsides and you fall back into the hammock
of another easy truth. There are so many ways to
disguise this. One reigning idea dictates what you will
think, and so you go blundering from one war to another,
one rape or abuse to another. My dream for you is clothed
with shadows. Listen,—your final dawn will arrive rudely.
What became of me wasn't worth the telling. But, I'll say
this: the real dungeons are our own words, the real chains
are the ones we use to encircle our own hearts. There are
letters in my alphabet you'll never know. I saw a whole
army collapse like a huge lung. I saw bodies fall like
chips from a woodsman's axe. There was a king who
believed me, and one who didn't. You know their fates.
Your own kings pencil in their beliefs for later erasure.
After each tragedy they hand out antique apologies.
Someone shoots in a theater and soon it plays like fiction.
Someone else pulverizes symbols they don't understand.
When you break the world it doesn't just get fixed.
You have no idea how many things you've become
a symbol for. Your answers explode like terrorist bombs.
There is a truth, if you listen, but it arrives with no
postmark and no return address, no provision for revision.
Even your windows mutter things you refuse to understand.
I can say: there is little patience with your skeletal words.
I can say: you should already know this by reading
what has already been written on the dungeon walls of
your own hearts and the watermarks of your own souls.
The harp plays on, but the question is, who's listening?

# The Secret Word: Lot's Wife

How could anyone not look back? I became the salt
of the earth, as your saying goes. But Lot never even
noticed me the next day. Salt of the earth. How could
anyone? The sun rose as usual. Cities shimmered
in the distance. I stood there like Eurydice as the earth
exploded. The sand is there only to explain the wind.
The hills ignore the valleys. The moon disowns its own
origins. The only life we have is history. But you are
afraid to look at your own past, your massacres for
your god or country, the hungry you ignore, the land
you kill. Salt of the earth. Next year's moths are waiting
in cocoons you nurtured yesterday. Who is anyone without
a desire to see what happens? You fill your clocks with
pictures that are out of focus. Everything you do provokes
the stars. That is why their cryptic alignments refuse
to give warnings. And the one word you have tried all
your lives to say dies on your lips as you die. It blows away
with the desert sand. Why do you believe your own words?
When was it your own Jesus called his disciples
the salt of the earth? My own names are on parole.
You turn your histories into anecdotes or slogans.
The horizon has crumbled. The weight of the sky is
nearly unbearable. All your signposts are blank.
The rags of forgotten flags litter your fathers' lands.
Your truth is what you believe, but it is only a distorted
carnival mirror. That's why there is always that unwanted
stranger, who looks away, lurking behind the subjects of
your photos. He steals the scene the way I steal your thoughts.
You say peace but mean war, love but mean power.
In the end you will forget your own names. Some
scribes have called me Edith. You can look it up.
It is just a word, and of no consequence. History says
I should warn you, and have. There. As if it would do
any good. Like me you'll turn and look. Like I did
you'll see only what you want to see. Salt of the earth.

# Nicodemus's Dream

Night was still dripping from the leaf tips.
I thought at first His words just littered
the ground. I had wanted to know
why we should believe anything
beyond the realm of the stars. All my dreams
belonged to someone else. What He gave me was
a way of dreaming from the insides of trees,
from the bottoms of clouds. It was like the lonely call
of the doves, the way the morning moon becomes
one with the sky. His words were metaphors
for other words, so that my dreams became
metaphors for other dreams. Every Religion is
a dream we try to believe. No way is really
the way. But I can tell you it is not any god's way
when you blow pieces of each other into bizarre
constellations. It is not anyone's word when
believers dream their own dreams as truths.
Each of those dreams only gives birth to another dream,
another beheading, or rape or gas attack.
If only we could hear the timeless echoes
that reach us from beyond the farthest ends
of the universe. Even your scientists know
they ride on gravity waves from the birth of everything.
It is a language of love giving birth to other loves.
Now I understand how each drop of rain must be
destined for its spot on the earth, how each shard of
sunlight must have a shadow to brighten. I am still
not sure what it is I heard Him say. You have to
doubt what you believe and believe what you doubt.
You have to work each long furrow of the heart whose
seeds will surprise you like the hidden stars of daylight.

# Elijah's Warning

Why does the soul, like a startled dove, flee from itself?
Why do we live so often in the dark caves of the heart?
These are the questions that nest like a tangle of spiders.
A man rises from the subway vent to a world that has
abandoned the world—to draw his lost life over a billboard
picture of a life he'll never know. Listen, there are storms
that shred mountains. There are rocks that shake themselves
as the earth splits. There are my words that you burned
to ashes now floating aimlessly. No one wanted to listen.
How easy it is to hope the clouds wash away the sky's light.
We have become so inventive in our cruelties—as today
a flash of shrapnel flies through a hospital ward, someone
drives a car into a crowd, a ISIS sniper welcomes the challenge
of a child's small head, another child is hollowed out by
a gang bullet from beyond her bedroom wall. No one wants
to listen. Ages ago I told the king what would happen.
Now, I'm telling you: your own kings are leading you
to dreams that are not dreams with words that are not words,
hopes that are not hopes. No one seems to understand
the shimmer of light that surrounds you before the lightning
strikes. Your excuses rise from the trees like vultures. No one
understands the script for their own roles drawn on abandoned
walls. But there's no language, no image that won't tell you what
I mean. Listen to the pain of the hills as they are torn apart
for a few dollars and whose veins are piped with poisons. Listen
to the cry of the child caught in the rubble of a suburban meth lab.
Listen: you have to hear more than you can hear. You can't really
understand until you hear the weight of pollen as it falls to earth,
the sound the moon makes dragging its pale, almost invisible
light, across the daytime sky, the way you push the air apart as you
walk, which is the soul's breath leaving or entering, which is
your breath as it sifts through the caves of your lungs. Listen.

# Obed's Warning

2 Chronicles 28:8

Even as I am talking to you someone spray paints
their belief on the walls of a bombed out building,
the city swifts knead the air into ominous flags,
a shift in the wind reminds you of the chemicals
we pass through like leaves on their way to the earth.
Even as I am talking a few more rumbles of tanks
ripple the water, patches of fog bruise the mountains,
someone attacks a church or a mosque, defaces
a temple or synagogue, brings the prisoners to be
executed in the name of one god or another.
I thought my words would be remembered.
There were two hundred thousand prisoners after
all that killing. What I said was forgiveness.
Even as they were for war I was for peace
as the Psalmist will tell you if you listen.
Sometimes the world seems so dark you have to
shut your eyes and wait till you can see the light.
How easy it is to stir all that into your coffee cup,
to write a few marginal notes on the blurred chronicle
of history. The world is more brittle than you think.
The peace I brought was no trick of light.
No one was guiltless then. No one ever is.
Everything exists in this one caged moment.
Soon enough every wall will crack. Soon enough
everyone wakes to the same light wrinkling the same
clouded horizon. The redbuds don't wait for the rest
to flower. The first stars don't wait for the others.
It is always a question of choice. Our shadows
don't know what it is they display. Even now
you kill what you fear, then fear what you kill.
Forget the cramped vision of the future. Especially now
take care that your words don't lose themselves
in the forest of what they cannot forgive, in what
could become, again, the burnt out roots of the soul.

# III

## BRIDGES

*Gone, lost, scattered to the four winds, it still surprises me how little now remains...*

—Wislawa Szymborska
"A Speech at the Lost and Found," *Map*

# Triptych

When you spin the globe
                       and touch that country,
it begins then for the child,
                       caught by chance
in a circular frame,
                       a tondo of sorts not unlike
those in the village church,
                       and unlike the windows
in the mosques, as he steps
                       out from behind the pocked
wall of what remains of
                       his house because it is dusk,
it is safe, and he can
                       almost taste the time,
can almost sense the few
                       shrewd stars waiting
to play their hand,
                       waiting as they do
in the enormous
                       loneliness of space that lies
beyond the broken
                       spines of trees the child
runs past for it is time
                       the game begins, not just
the football on the dust lot,
                       but the one seen
through the scope,
                       that is of the Zastava M48
with its 7.92X57 mm
                       load, nestled as it is
on its tripod, delicate
                       as the legs of a spider,
blackened so as to avoid
                       reflecting any revealing light
there, on the mountain that is
                       more like the spine of this

camouflaged man nestled out of sight,
                    a long but not impossible
shot, like unraveling
                    a rope until it is
taut, but now there is no
                    need to range or adjust
for wind, a wind that
                    hardly whispers
its warnings, above
                    the scratching of the
ground birds or secrets of
                    the hawk, no need now
to pull the trigger because yes,
                    now the boy steps, without
looking, and knows
                    before he hears
the land mine's click crumbling
                    into its own distant echo
as the light crumbles
                    through the trees and he
himself now seems
                    to know he is not there,
not here, while the other
                    gently removes the scope,
rises, leaves, carries
                    the Zastava as you would
a child, for he knows,
                    no need to look now,
knows already how the boy
                    has become smudged against
the sky, a kind of red scar
                    spreading mid-air,
and if you yourself looked
                    closely through the scope
known for its clumsy
                    design, the tonda

seems to quiver, and you
                              yourself can see now
the child's dreams shredded
                              as he himself is
shredded, as the light is
                              shredded,  a prism effect,
a light-show swelling
                              the air,—blossoming,—
a Calla lily on fire
                              as—colorless—the other
children freeze even
                              in this late hot sun,
afraid to step, wanting
                              to be lifted out, angel,
helicopter, an epidemic
                              of clocks turning too
fast, or broken, stuttering,
                              yours, the heart's
aftershocks, love's aftershocks,

                              *

                              and those shocks that begin again
with your finger nudging
                              the heart's tectonic plates
hidden beneath the continents
                              on the globe in front of
you with its colorful spectrum
                              of countries, the same
spectrum you gazed at
                              in the school lab as the light
split itself apart through
                              the pyramid prism and you
wondered how complex
                              each simple thing could be,
and you pointed to where
                              years later—(which is now

in time's twisted syntax),—
                              you could hear hushed syllables
echoing unwanted meanings,
                              but the child, low light
slashing through him, through
                              a stand of live oak, reddish,
for the sun has begun
                              to burrow into the hidden horizon,
  as if the whole world were
                              dying around him, the brush
decorated with thorns,
                              stones that scar the land,
hears a rumor of something
                              he doesn't yet understand,
shadows moving on their own,
                              bird song without the birds,
roots sinking too deep
                              to follow, and his own dreams,
there in the background
                              like a swarm of yellow jackets
or the low hum of the interstate
                              but, no, that is too distant
to hear,—the world now
                              becoming less believable,
the backbone of the ridgeline
                              wanting to turn into darkness
itself, there, where another man
                              watches, remembering a
tortured light, a dozen
                              headlights creating a stage,
a medieval play, a game,
                              back then, masked, hooded,
the bonfire tossing light
                              against the live oak trees
that still grab the air
                              with their careless branches,

as they grabbed, carelessly,

                    those lives he still doesn't know,

but where the child now

                    hesitates, watches, yes, as if

looking at an earthen tondo—if

                    he knew the name,—painted by

hate, like looking through

                    those kaleidoscope tubes

you did as a child yourself

                    amazed, but here you are

looking into the past

                    that swirls dizzily,

a catacomb of ghosts,

                    a honeycomb of knifed

ideas, leprous light,

                    for back then darkness covered

the darkness, but now

                    this tortured silence of

a rotten rope slung over

                    a rotten branch, an image

from a story that had been

                    only a story, a dream

that hangs there, empty,

                    imagined, but also visible

as the sides hanging

                    in the butcher shop or

the deer strung up for

                    cleaning, still wondering

how it came here, or as

                    the white laundry sheets gesturing

from backyard clothes lines

                    like signal flags revealing how

once they could have been

                    hoods, so, yes, he knows

that, and so knows better

                    than the other, knows why

the hands of the town
                              clock point always away
from the moment, accuse time
                              itself of forgetting, like posters
thinking always of the future,
                              not drilling into the past
as he is now, memories
                              stuttering, crumbling
in his hands, wonders
                              when he will stop living
those undreamt dreams

                              *

                              or it begins again, the silhouette
against the blinds where
                              the light fingers the globe
to where the sound oozes
                              through, more than sound,—
a window, movie screen,
                              gallery frames of crucifixions,
a threat, what you dream
                              alone in the woods at night,
moon wrapped in gauze,
                              the trail melted away long ago,
so the child in this case
                              hesitates now, his soul looking
desperately around
                              to be somewhere else,
drops the flowers, more
                              weed than flower, the way
Adam did at Eve's approach,
                              that loss of innocence,
a loneliness like a single
                              bell rope in the abandoned
clock tower of the church,
                              its steeple pointing towards

the emptiness of space
                    the child fills with imagination,
the heart blindfolded,
                    a children's story, but now no longer
at the helm, now being the wrong
                    knight, unhorsed, the wrong
maiden won, all these
                    stories once read to him
in a cotton light, lost now,
                    those days of games before
the man's terrifying arrival
                    that circles him like starlings
as he passes the collapsed
                    stone wall, the car up on blocks,
and sees the woman's face
                    a jigsaw puzzle of scars,
the man's shadow
                    flailing in the blinds,
the music a loud glove
                    pressed over her mouth,
the child knowing who is
                    next, but hesitating
this one time, dreaming
                    a sky all his own, a door
only he can open, a path
                    quickly covered behind him
with time's leaves because
                    there are no words for this,
just his feelings uncoiling
                    among the faintest stars, a kite
cut loose, a hawk floating
                    as if on some invisible lake,
because it is about what is
                    missing, what the stream
running over the cliff
                    wants to fill, dusk

like a puddle filling
                      the valley, the catbird
raiding anyone's nest,
                      bats returning to the cave,
water filling the eye's
                      ducts, because he hesitates, yes,
to leave her here, the air
                      made suddenly of stone, night
snaking towards him
                      through the trees,—the threat, the door,
the sky, the loneliness,—
                      and so what do you tell him, what
do you tell any of them,
                      for it is you, no, we who have scoped
this out here, shadowed
                      their shadows, wandered among
their dreams, as if
                      they were not our own,
as if the mockingbird
                      did not imitate this voice
we ourselves invent, singing,
                      from his hidden branch as if
the dust of our lives did not
                      fall into the eyes of the dead,
as if our own soul might
                      finally pass through the tiny
tondo of a needle' s eye,
                      though it may be that it cannot help
bringing night with it,
                      bringing these words falling into
themselves, standing as we are,
                      here, at dusk's boundary line.

# Waking, a Question

*...it is possible*
*to offer to the betrayed world*
*a rose*
—Zbigniew Herbert

Maybe the way the first light
               rubs the dew off the window,
the sky opening to whatever is
               beyond sky, the path that is
not a path redrawing itself,
               the morning doves questioning
what they have whispered
               to each other, but really
it is that light, the way
               it enters like a rival to touch
your forehead, a doctor
               checking for fever, the way
it approaches like a distant
               sound, a bell ring rising out of
the shadows, that are
               themselves becoming just
an idea of shadow,
               crickets having finished
questioning who they are,
               the leaves of the redbud
clutching the first flashes,
               the owl sending out its last
pleas as if there were
               no end to them, no end
to the aroma of dew
               on the switch grass filling
the air, all these things
               that make you turn, half
asleep, half conscious,
               like the fish that once passed
unseen beneath our canoe,
               and then to wander off
for a moment that is
               hardly a moment, to question

who it is here beside you
            who has arrived out of
so many years, a kind of
            fog that fingers its way
across a river's surface,
            hiding the splash of
the otter who is surprised
            as we are, the splash of
oarlocks from someone
            out early, and then
the splash of a lure
            as he finishes his cast,
or it is the memory of
            sound, not the sound, like
your grandfather whispering
            to the chicken some
consolation before he swings
            her in one hand by
the neck because she has
            not been laying, but
because it is not the death,
            it is the life, no end to it,
what approaches
            with the radiance
now at dawn's precipice
            there on the far ridge,
remembered and questioned,
            the valley pulling itself
out through the pass
            on the other side where
we walked once, and
            the waterfall, that summer
heat, barely a pencil line
            trying to write a future,
even in these times,
            for it is now the questions swarm

like remembered nightmares
                        where suddenly the sky seems
to press heavily down on
                        the wren's song just beginning
impossible among the distant
                        messages spray painted on
the wreckage of walls
                        some army left behind,
no end to their horrors,
                        claiming a return, a revision,—
but if only this were
                        a poem where the leaf can
hang mid-air for a lifetime,
                        where the child soldiers of
Asia and Africa can drop
                        their Kalashnikovs that
stand taller than they are,
                        or where the girls can keep
returning from Boko Haram
                        though for them the sky will be
always ripped open, but
                        the question this morning is
not how to erase this
                        phalanx of images that have
broken out of our nightmares
                        but how to correct the things
themselves, the boy crucified
                        to the door in Bosnia, the beheaded
Christians, the limbless
                        children of Aleppo, no end to them,
as I hear the muted sounds
                        of boxcars coupling nightly
in the train yard conjuring up
                        the distant sounds of artillery
that haunted me nightly
                        those days during the war,

conjuring the same question
                          again—that is, is it possible
to love the world for we can
                          only sense an answer
like knowing the stars
                          as Braille dots, listening
as if for the first time to
                          the mornings' dew dripping
one into another without
                          the muzzle flash, the macheted
slogans, but only the heart's
                          landscape, as it was questioned,
and that is it, isn't it,
                          the need for something
eternally circling, not
                          a helicopter blade, not some
drone stalking us, but
                          maybe like a swift returning
each night to its chimney
                          of dreams, its private sky,
or maybe like this ceiling
                          fan, circling its eternal question,
or a distant moon, like
                          the kind of curved question mark
science describes space as,
                          a receding only to return,
to the future that abandoned
                          nests in our redbud must really mean
appearing again in that same
                          tree, under the same sky,
and light too, this light,
                          bending, becoming its own
reflection, as this dream is
                          yours now, mine, barely known,
empty vase, the possible
                          flash of a wing in the tree

if that's what it was,

     invisible sound in the brush,
stars that turn slowly off

     each dawn so that we begin
to see how many things

     can go on living without us,
the words of prophets that try

     to pray what cannot be thought,
no end to it, the new planets

     that seem a swirl of vapor,
imagined shapes on the sky's

     horizon, so that it seems
we already exist in an afterlife,

     afterlight, whatever has been
waiting to surface after

     last night's rain, all these
things becoming a part

     of us, the butterfly that
drinks from the empty

     half of a robin's egg
that has fallen just outside

     the window, the whole
garden that has risen

     at your touch, these things
that give time to the earth,

     the soul, a kind of love
that you can hear whispering

     from the farthest points
in space, invisible

     gravitational waves that
give weight to the heart,

     that tell us we are moving
as the day moves through

     the trees, as even the air
seems to ripen, every insect

     floating through its own echoes,

the whole world adrift,
                              these questions, too, taking shape
on your face, indelible now,
                              as you open your eyes
like an embrace because
                              one love leads to another,
one word begins to answer
                              another, becoming a poem,
this one, perhaps, climbing
                              its own broken lines,
as the caterpillar climbs,
                              blindly, but not without hope,
from his own betrayed world
                              slowly up the tattered screen
whose cross stitches blanket us,
                              crawls slowly towards
another body, another sky,
                              an embrace of Love that is this one.

# String Theory

In my dream of it nothing is
        where it should be. The puzzle of the horizon
            shatters. We gather the pieces.
Wood moths try to fill the spaces between
        branches. The bulbs we planted
            have already broken through.
Is this a dream or a memory? The wind stretches
        itself into a thin string that wraps itself
            around these words. Clouds
wrinkle like crepe paper. No, this must be a memory.
        A swing saying *yes* then *no* from
            the bomb's concussion.
What bomb? There were too many to count, too
        many places it fell. Its own words
            not yet invented. These dreams
sleep like palimpsests in ancient manuscripts.
        Not even the monks deciphered them.
            Did I say dreams? Is this the past
or the future? Moles keep burrowing their ancient
        questions in the yard outside. All right,
            then, this is now. Riding over
the potholes of memory The beginning never ends.
        The end is sealed. We put the best face
            on it, invent a new mask of words.
Climbers know, only the crampons hide the secret
        of the rock face. The world is everything
            that is the world, one philosopher
says. The universe is a hologram we keep copying from
        one generation to the next, another says.
            We don't see what it is we are.
In a few millennia the sun will sift its ashes through
        whatever is left of wherever we were.
            The moon will shatter like one of
those Sweetgum pods. That is no dream. It is
        a memory pasted in the heart's scrapbook.
            Hartley thought our dreams were

the heart's garbage dump. There are two owls outside
taunting each other which is neither dream
nor memory. It is now, when far from
here someone has driven a car into a crowd to say
something he doesn't understand. *You have
to learn to love him if you hope to
ever stop the death of your own heart,* someone prayed
later from the crowd. And so it is, only now
do I begin to see how all this is
connected. The past is always something just pending.
Every moment strays into another history.
In this way, too, the heart echoes
its own forgotten stories, as this evening, what prompted
all this—the fading, high pitched scream of
the rabbit some coyote had carried away,
the sound knifing its way through these memories,
through the tendons of lost words that showed
a way to love, finally, this flawed world.

# IV

## OUR OWN DISTANCES

*We are reading the story of our lives*
*as though we were in it...*
　　　　—Mark Strand
　　　　　　"The Story of Our Lives," *Collected Poems*

# Not The Words

Maxine Kumin,  d. 2014


It is not the stars but the dark spaces between them
that haunt me. When I heard, the crows lining the empty
branches looked down in disbelief. It was like trying to find
where the wind goes. Every word is a sieve that never holds
what we need. I remember how the next morning the horses
at Reflection Riding stood pointing in the same direction.

It is never our lives but what our lives want to say to us.
At these times we need our shadows to point a way out
of ourselves. Every word is entangled in every other word.
The early light seems to raffle whatever I say here. I remember
how you worried that your horses would trample your dog,
the way your voice created not only words but the heart's music.

It is not through words but through those lost notes of the heart
that we find a way. In every shift of the wind some shadow of
a soul quivers. Every word hopes to believe in a single other word.
This morning the crows don't know what to say or dream.
It is not by the stars but by what they hide that we define
our words. This morning the horses scatter as the wind turns.

# Traces

Remembering Tomas Tranströmer

Not like Zechariah who became mute because he didn't
believe the angel's words. But instead, those few dates
traced in the table dust at the outdoor café, birthdates,
it turned out, for friends we might have in common. A few
years after the stroke. How does anyone not feel shuttered
at that? The sky was a mirror for what we never said.
Our words exist only for what is absent. Our loves exist
because the moonlight evaporates before we can hold it.
Sunlight splintered on the clouds. Our own reflections,
traced on the surface, continued downstream somewhere.
The roads, too, never agree on any destination. So it seemed
the moment we were waiting for got mislaid. It arrives now,
too late, as I am listening to your left hand piano that flutters,
a hummingbird questioning a flower, threading through
the heart with the silent language that angel would understand.

# Apricot Pits: A Story

for Metka Krašovec

How often something seems to open the gate of the mind
and introduce itself when you expected another visitor.
Like the image of that gardener lining up apricot pits
on the casement of his wall, and offering me the fruit
over the garden gate—but I had wanted to start with
another scene, the fortified church at Hrastovlje, Slovenia,
just up the hill from us, a refuge from Turkish raids
centuries ago. We were standing there where two worlds,
two tectonic plates were colliding beneath us, one slipping
under the other imperceptibly except for occasional
earthquakes now and then, but that is not the story here.
I wanted to write how I came for the frescoes, long hidden,
*The Dance of Death*, peasant to Bishop lined up on a wall
for their interview with Death, and how I came for a prayer.
Above them, creation frescoes on the ceiling seemed to linger
beyond their seven days as if to delay what the pilgrims
were headed for. A year earlier I lost a daughter and now
I feared a dear friend had started her own long dance
in a hospital not far from there with yet another treatment.
The day's heat revealed itself as a haze on the far cliffs.
The meadow grass was already browned. I remembered
then how apricot pits contain Laetrile, a kind of
last judgment treatment for cancer, and a poison,
which is why the gardener was removing the pits and
chasing the squirrels from eating them. *Živeljenje,*
he had said, or *zanživete, Life,* or *coming into life,*
what the church was trying to teach but what the gardener
seemed to teach so much better. Each apricot seemed to
shine like its own sun and world, like the many worlds
science says we inhabit, or will inhabit after all is done.
What could I tell my friend except how I walked around
the fortress walls to a path leading nowhere but where
it leads, which is where you want it to lead, beyond
the world you think you know, a world whose deadly
pits are seeds that bring forth new trees, new life,
*zanživete,* to everything we thought would disappear.

# Chattanooga, 16 July 2015

The crepe myrtle no longer means what it did
yesterday. The clouds refuse to move on. A single
dog barks in the distance but doesn't know why.
A slight wind blows a door open but no one's there.
It is as if the souls of the dead hushed the earth's
spin. Beyond the ridge, the river whispers its own
lament. Our words are broken bridges. Tonight
I've been fingering my father's gold oak leaf Major's
pin by a small light, trying desperately to expand
the garden. The cicadas stop, then start, hesitating.
He used to call them crickadees. What they say,
he said, was a prayer that needed no words.
The mockingbird in an upper branch must know
some secret the evening is hiding. A few pools
of light linger over the ridge. One star pokes through,
then another joins it, either in consolation or in prayer.

# Dawn on Amelia Island

Remembering Mark Strand

You can see through the sea oats, swaying as if
to escape or embrace the offshore breeze,
the freighter laden with stories we will never read.
Beyond the horizon *Dark Harbors* have begun
to appear. A few charcoaled branches still try
to capture the night from someone's cold fire pit.
A hermit crab scuttles looking for a shell to claim
as its own. The early fishermen are casting
for sand sharks. The breakwater doesn't fool
the tides. The history here seems eaten by
sea worms. It was here that the slaves died
of cancers from harvesting the indigo plants
for a few bright colors of cloth beyond
that horizon. The ships that carried their human
cargo have long ago sunk. *A few clouds bleed,*
you wrote. We only want *not to be left behind.*
And now, the morning light seems to explode
out of a live oak. Time is a verb with no subject.
Like the cosmic rays that pass through us every
minute. In the meantime the earth rotates a few
miles, and inches further along in its orbit,
leaving behind so few of our words.

# The Mudpuddle

Remembering Aleš Debeljak, Ljubljana

It exists only in the mudpuddle just as Escher saw
another world at the bottom of his painting,
but here now, 8,000 miles from you, where
the moon tries desperately to reflect its reasons,
where the cat comes to sip and turns away,
where the tracks leading away disappear after
a few steps, where the sun now seems to only
paint shadows of tree limbs, and a few
passers-by who avoid the puddle, as it slips
down behind a hill, but not your shadow
which has wandered off without you into
its own darkness from the Peračica Viaduckt
where rope jumpers used to free fall into another
world, as above them the paragliders turned pages
of the wind writing new stories with each turn,
and beneath it all the tiny stream still cuts into
the rock on its desperate journey that knows no end.

# Fog Rises from the Leaves

Remembering Tomaž Šalamun

Through the barren tree limbs and the fog
that lingers like a half-remembered thought,
the moon is a bright smudge that hides
whatever stars were around it. But nothing is
ever where or when we see it. I remember
the flashlights fingering their way through
ground fog as we searched for Ludwig.
Lipica. When was that? Leaves are scattered
on the ground like unused words.
Gravitational waves bend the light, and time.
Maybe that is why the child asked today,
*when we lose time can we find it later?*
Tonight it is almost two years.
Galaxies continue to flow in currents
and swirl in eddies like pools of water
the child was playing in.
There's a face in every word we remember.
That's why your own words echo here tonight.
*Megla se dviga iz listja. Fog rises from the leaves.*
*Utrujen sem biti sam. I am tired of being alone.*
Every word has a future tense the way Zechariah's
horses and trees stood for future worlds he couldn't see.
Today we are still trying to map the cosmos
though its pages are smeared with theories.
And who are we but metaphors for what we want to be?

# Spooky Action at a Distance: an Elegy

Franz Wright 1953-2015

That woman, olive army jacket loose over her Salvation Army
skirt, has coaxed her shopping cart towards whatever life
the morning might bring. A few blackbirds are still trying
to deny the dawn. A dragonfly stops mid-air to imagine
a life beyond this one, then darts away as if to forget it.
Isn't that bee trying to sip from the soda can a bit pretentious?
The woman's dreams are bottomless. How does the woodpecker
know where to strike next? How does one distant atom know
what the other is doing? How does the wind that has come
such a long way know which windows to rattle? The stars have
already dissolved. Our dreams are locked under eyelids.
The distant mountains appear like hedges. The pale moon is
humbled. Birds celebrate the fact of air. Franz would know that
God sits around the fire under the overpass with the other migrant
workers. Their souls are made of blood. Anything that's anything
seems out of reach. If only he could supply their papers. If only
the day delivered on its promises. Eternity's mirror reflects us all.
It doesn't matter that the skywriter's message is already tattered.
A truck jackknifes. A train totters off the tracks. The woman knows
more than we do about pilgrimage. The workers know which
prayers are real and which aren't. The long narrow streaks of cloud
stretch towards the horizon as if some giant hand had reached
up from the earth and scratched the sky trying to get out.

# Poem for Amy

Some days the doves seemed to know
what we needed to know. Some days
you would run until you fell into the air,
and the birds would scatter like clouds.

What is it you were wanting to hold there
in your empty hand? I think you were starting
to play, even then, your flute, hearing
the strange music of the doves, the notes

floating feather-like into the future. And what
does a single feather mean except the love
we treasure, or a butterfly mean except
the dreams we chase, the way those doves

chased whatever called them from beyond the park,
something beyond words, beyond the sky
that gives away nothing except the longing
to discover how love creates its own endless skies.

# The Doors of the Heart

A sequence in response to Metka Krašovec's drawings
related to Emily Dickinson

## 1. THE SHEATH

With every errant word there is a ripple of gravitational
waves that brush, unheard, against us. We want to
command the wind to follow one path. The rudder of
dusk is broken. We sheathe our dreams. Nobody is attached.
Everyone fears their own space. We think our words
believe in us. We think a crutch of light will poke down
through the clouds. Instead, eternity drips down the gutters.
One idea forgets what the other idea wanted to whisper.
Still, each self tries to discover its other shedded selves.
The clock, meanwhile, borrows its time from the heart.

## 2. ABYSS

Does a dead star still claim what light abandoned it?
What is out of sight hijacks the truth. Memories mold
in dungeon light. The heart flies off into another
abyss. A spiteful moon offers no consolation. Deep
in the iris of each eye someone is beheaded, another
dumped into a ditch or explodes in a marketplace
thinking they are a supernova. How seldom the light
keeps its promise. You have to stretch the sky to survive.
Above, fireflies breathe like so many floating lungs.
No scream is loud enough. A blind cosmos sails on.

## 3. THE VEIL

Sometimes all we had were fishermen's handlines to connect us.
Sometimes we'd search for shells of horseshoe crabs we imagined
as skulls tucked into tidal flats. Gulls poked at whatever tumbled
out of the waves. I remember a dingy just offshore guided by a body
they didn't let us see. Sometimes a whole sky can appear in a patch
of ocean. Beyond what we know there is a whole harvest of stars
we hope exist. No one believed the story that the gulls were disguised
angels. Prayers, however, opened like mussel shells. Replicas of
ourselves tumbled through the immense vacuums of space. Words
swung into orbit around us but sent no signals, and still don't land.

## 4. SAFE DESPAIR

There are wounds whose roots entangle our words for them.
There are blades whose tongues eat the ashen air.
There are sails that refuse the wind, untold despairs
that straddle the earth, horrors whose tentacles are endless.
There are warped skies, islands of shadow that are
your only hope. There are hours that have no measure.
There are thorns your fingers become out of prayer.
There is the earth you become trying to grow out of yourself.

## 5. BREATH

Each dream carves its own cave into the wind.
Each breath you draw is a borrowed sky.
Every flower is a mystery. Clouds are gnostic.
The heron is the key. Trout are false leads.
In Mumbai words floated around us like gnats.
Gnats, too, are a key. The heron floats like
A string bow. Your hands pray the same as the sky.
Any time now the answer steps out of the cave.

## 6. EVERY GRIEF

In winter the squirrel nests appear clamped to bare branches.
You can feel gravity making its claims. Grief gnaws your dreams.
The script of your heart is unreadable. Your hopes are inverted
candles that spread ashes over the canvas of your life. There is
no path you haven't explored, no driftwood you've found which
brings a hope you could measure. Still, a sacred vision seems to
lounge over every despair. The soul hovers as if to question the grief
you've etched into your eyes. The mind has a plumbline to measure this.

## 7. FROM NOWHERE

For that one moment we live where the sky becomes sea
and the sea becomes sky. For that one moment no owl
speaks, no cricket chants. No wave breaks on the rocks.
We begin to forget the reality of things. We walk as if
without shadows, unseen by all we see. Everything is
only itself and reveals nothing. Our words are dusk.
From nowhere comes the clicking of a freight train
on the tracks. It ships one darkness into another.
How many sentences have we used to describe what
we could not describe. Only in a labyrinth of shapes
can we see who we are. Light spills over the horizon
and starts to rise like the tide, lighting the ashen air
as it rises. It files no report, nor any hints of its travels.

## 8. THE WOUND

Sometimes the soul ignites from within the body.
It dances with words we long ago closed our ears to.
How many times has the soul become like the dead
space between walls. The shotgun my father carried
seemed to tear open the air, but the imagined sound was
louder. There is an irretrievable sadness in every love.
He never shot anything except his own heart. We knelt
once beside an abandoned kill. You could see heaven
in his eyes. At dawn the face of a cloud blushed with love.

## 9. OCCULSIONS

A December moon that erases Venus nightly.
Cosmic dust gathering in the heart's corners.
The whole sky turning away. The lake refusing
to reflect it. A world of fractals and blind birds
shattering the windows. The simple pleasure
meteors display penciling towards the horizon.
You have to turn around to see them all.
Otherwise all futures are recurrent tragedies,
all plans will only splatter the paper with
fragments of desperation. Each word a telescope,
each breath a hyphen, each love a question.
You have to let your sentences end with commas.

## 10. NO DIRECTION

You can see in the overturned stump of the giant oak
how many directions the roots explore. The tiny finch
on the fallen branch wants to fly everywhere at once.
I have been watching the cat try to guess what entrance
the mole will make. There are no maps or blueprints
for the heart. It is like trying to figure why the river cut
its ravine here rather than there. Our own choices hover
behind us. Too easily we board up our dreams. Kafka
waited for a lifetime before a door he could have opened.
How many loves have burrowed into the recesses of the mind?
The key is what you write when you write with the heart.

## 11. PRIMED

There are only so many words between you and your death.
Someone beyond the end of your life keeps watch over you.
In the end you are the corporate story someone has written.
Your past haunts the corners with the other spiders. You have
to leave words like breadcrumbs to find your way back.
Darkness blows in like a sandstorm. A crow flicks a wing
and floats against the black sun. And so the heart is primed.

# Behind the Eight Ball

It's the way the six ball glances off the four and finds
its way to the side pocket is how Brother Linus explained it
in 1960, meaning how the halfback hits the hole then bounces
outside. Or it's the way one atom hits another and causes
a chain reaction was what the Brother we called "Red"
tried to tell us a few years later, explaining how this led
finally to Hiroshima's melting. Everything we know is just
a metaphor, Meister Eckhart wrote in 1303.
                                    Which is why
we can say the green felt surface of the table is like
the surface of a pond, and that we just sail from one rack
to another. Every metaphor controls us unawares.
*A dead shot* we say, not thinking what that could mean.
Or what we mean when we say how some militia runs
the table on a village.
                        It's when we believe our metaphors
that we are in trouble, turning them into facts like the way
John Wier in 1564 calculated confidently that there were
7 Million, 409 thousand, 127 demons working for Lucifer
under the middle management of 79 demon princes leading
to lots of bodies left smoldering at stakes or hung on wheels.
Or how the skull was thought, in Neolithic times, to be
the sacred source of the soul, which explains why they were
staked on castle walls so the victors could trap their spirits
and which led later to the guillotine. Every metaphor has
a history we hardly understand.
                                How did we get here?—
Of course: the chain reaction metaphor, bank shots, miscues,
the way we are always behind the eight ball of one
fanatic or another—some madman in Syria or warlord
in Africa, maybe a disgruntled employee with a gun and an idea.
This is when the surface of our lake rebels against its depths,
shivers for the lost stories flooded like towns beneath it.
                                                You have

to play the angles, trace the trajectory off the diamonds
several collisions ahead to leave the cue where you'll be

set up to finish. There's no playing safe. Tonight a few reflected
meteors scratch the fabric of the lake's surface. You think
that's just an embellishment to fill the space? Every metaphor
refers to something we can't say. The blue chalk clings
to your fingers like history. We'd like to think it's only just
a game, and then, before you know it, it's your turn to break.

# Complaint of the Muse

I've read the stories. A hooded sky. Orphaned stars.
The trees doubtful. Words stagnating like rainwater
in a ditch. The guilty evening putting on its gloves.
Stories like thieves that stalk you under a tattler's moon.
We follow our shadows until they become the night.
So there's no way I'm staying inside this poem without
a few changes. Each time I let an image out the door
someone smothers it. Each time I lean against a wall
someone starts throwing knives. Someone else
hacks off the limbs of whoever gave comfort to an enemy.
Nero used to use Christians as human torches at his feasts.
Why bring all this into this flea market of a poem?
Why can't the poet just focus on how the moon keeps
tracing its finger on the sky without asking a question.
Why can't he just talk about his love whose every glance is
like a first raindrop on the cheek? Or her smile the wind blows in?
What about the comic scene where the wild horse chased them
across the desert in Arizona? Now he tells us that Kierkegaard
called the moon our conscience. The air shivers. There's
another war with new weapons to test already buying tickets
for another country. Sometimes the world is only a mirage.
I try to supply the useless facts that will distract him.
It is only when our words are disfigured that we know what
they meant. Mongols invented lemonade in the 13th Century.
Influenza comes from the Italian because of the influence
stars were thought to have on our health. The House
of Mysteries in Pompey should occupy him for a long time.
So much sex. Everyone inventing their own god.
Sardonic grin comes from the way Homer thought Sardinians
smirked. In the meantime he's writing about Malalai Kakar,
murdered by the Taliban for trying to save girls from forced
marriages. Why won't he listen to me? The clock keeps
starting over as if it could get things right with another try.
We all want to think we are irreplaceable. *Even Asparagus
inspires thought*, wrote Charles Lamb. Every poem is a lie,
wrote Fernando Pessoa. Someone's being taken away.
I don't think I can stop what's coming next. See, now,
the way he cuts me off as if I were the knife at his throat?

# It Is if You Say It Is

I had almost forgotten my life as a constellation
until the ray from the lighthouse, wobbling like
the beam from those colliding stars burning out
eons ago, and leaving a black hole, brought it all
back. Originally, I compared that black hole
to a an abandoned campfire but Pam and Bill
thought that was too much of a stretch. But then
what should I do with the image of the hiker
who passes by and remembers his own burnt
down house? Nothing I guess. Let's move on.
You can't just carbon date a memory like that.
It's like a mysterious note tucked in an old Bible
some relative left for who knows whom. This
explains why the air today is so metaphysical.
Dawn steps down. Night raises its head. This is
Time's ruthless floor plan. We are all punching-in
for the last shift, Phil mused, and not a moment too soon.
For years Tomaž refused to open his Chinese fortune
cookie hoping to hold off the future he couldn't hold off.
Nowadays they are mostly stuffed with silly slogans.
We must love one another *and* die, wrote Auden,
revising the choice he gave us in his first version.
Derrida says we wrote before we spoke. See, I told you
today is metaphysical. Charlemagne is responsible
for the script we use that separates words. But we still
hardly understand each other. Words mean anything
you want them to mean, no more, no less, said Alice's
White Rabbit. In Cherokee, the first woman's name is
also the name for corn. Pharmacy comes from the Greek,
meaning both poison and cure. *The quick brown fox
jumps over a lazy dog* is a panagram, meaning it uses
all the letters of the alphabet, which is not to say it is
not true. You can stone some peaches, but you shouldn't
stone your neighbor (even if he says he likes to get stoned).
Why is it that all elegies are love poems, and all love poems
elegies? In the end, we are just looking for a human feeling.
Sometimes it is impossible to decipher the tone of an e-mail.

No one has yet deciphered the strange prehistoric
Rongorongo script of Easter Island. Its heaven-looking
statues aren't saying a thing. Neither are the stone saints
wandering around Italy with their lifelines to another
world. I haven't talked to my angel in days. Nightingale,
when will your song fly beyond the world we know?
You need words for that kind of love, but there aren't any.
They dissolve like the stardust that falls around us each day.
There are things we never forget and things we must never
know, will never know. Even the most trivial things are
metaphysical. Take for example my dog, Wilbur.
It's important for *her* world that she knows where to pee.
And why does the campfire smoke always blow towards
me? We are floating on the sea surface of space with
no light to guide us. *These late eclipses of the sun and
moon*, lamented Gloucester. And what should we make
of the hundreds of ancient stone gates discovered in
the Saudi desert and leading to nothing at all? The whole
planet is riding like driftwood towards the shores of
another galaxy. Is that why the moon is stalking us?
If light really does bend will it circle back to its beginnings?
Why does the trail of string always end before the end?
How do those deep-sea creatures produce their own
light? Like them, we live in one of those snow globes.
I still can't figure out if that is a metaphor or a reality.
My students say *Mother!* is a film whose metaphor
describes Eden. Someone else says it's Satan's version
of events. The heart of one character is torn open
to mean God's beginning. I'm opting out of that meaning.
You can put anything next to anything and someone
will tell you what it means. The world is a place where
truths dream we know about them. The heron floating
over the river like a divining rod. Not to mention, the owl
smacking into the sky, an optical illusion maybe.
The wooden warbler on my desk wants to flap away
the pesky gnats that have suddenly flown in through
the open window. And how about Jim writing about the trout

that bit him while washing the dishes? What are the chances?
I miss Jim, too. There's no way to avoid the past tense.
Our dreams traipse about the streets on scraps of paper.
There are just too many hurts I want to bubble wrap
with these clouds of forgetfulness. I called Gerry just
to see if he was alive after the news of Phil. The heart's
dam bursts at these farewells. Dean's heart is not
his heart. What are those chances? He thinks we are all
just celestial debris. Maybe we should be listening
to the static that comes from, well, —remember those
dead stars at the beginning? Too often our lives are like
those old silent movies. Everyone busy looking at
their phones. It won't be long before we turn into
electronic signals like the woman in *Lucy* who turned
herself into electrons. She's there every time we turn on
the light. Is there any way to ever tell the whole story?
All that was left of the bicyclist yesterday was a chalk outline
on the road. Time's a custodian who never sweeps away
everything he sees. We get worried the constellations will
keep drifting apart and become new gods. That's why
we keep lighting the church candles that burn down.
Now the clock is searching for an extra number. This is
the only prayer I could muster before it turned elegy.
Who's left? The stars don't care for our geometry. I wish
I had enough time to mention everyone I loved. Beyond
that lighthouse, by mid-air, the dolphin has seen enough.

Special thanks to Stephen Corey, Sascha Feinstein, Josh Mensch, Pam Uschuk and Bill Root for their support, to Sarah Simmons and Mackenzie Scott for their help, and to my students at UTC and VCFA for inspiring me by the example of their good work. Thanks also to the Slovene Writers' Association for a Dane Zajc Residency, and to Iztok Osojnik for a writing residency in Škocjan, Slovenia.

RICHARD JACKSON is the author of fourteen books of poems, most recently *Out of Place* (2014, rpt. 2017) from Ashland Poetry Press, *The Hearts' Many Doors* (anthology, 2017) and *Retrievals* (2015), as well as ten books of criticism, anthologies and translations. He is a winner of Guggenheim, Fulbright, NEA, NEH, Witter-Bynner fellowships, five Pushcart Prize appearances, the Dane Zajc residency in Slovenia, and the Order of Freedom medal from the President of Slovenia for humanitarian and literary work during the Balkan wars.

CPSIA information can be obtained
at www.ICGtesting.com
Printed in the USA
BVHW03s0048090218
507710BV00001B/91/P

9 781941 209721